Pig *and the* Accidental OiNK!

PICTURE BOOK APOLOGETICS *with* JAMES & RUTH

by J.D. CAMORLINGA

Picture Book Apologetics, Whittier 2013

Printed in the United States of America

First Printing, 2013

All scripture quotations, unless otherwise indicated, are taken from the Holy Bible, New International Version®, NIV®. Copyright ©1973, 1978, 1984, 2011 by Biblica, Inc.™ Used by permission of Zondervan. All rights reserved worldwide. www.zondervan.com The "NIV" and "New International Version" are trademarks registered in the United States Patent and Trademark Office by Biblica, Inc.™

ISBN 978-0615878621

Picture Book Apologetics
Whittier, CA

www.PictureBookApologetics.com

ACKNOWLEDGEMENTS

We give all glory to the Father who created us, to the Son who redeemed us and to the Spirit who sealed us; Praise be to Him!

DEDICATION

For James, our beloved son, who is proof of a promise fulfilled, and for inquisitive young minds everywhere. May you grow to love God and be confident that what you believe is true!

James and Ruth love to play outside.

Each morning in the sunshine, and even in the rain, they run and jump and hide and seek, and thank God for the good things He made.

Sometimes, when they feel small because everything is just so beautiful and just so big, they holler "**God is GOOD**," because He made the sunshine and the rain, and He made their bodies to run and jump and hide and seek.

One day, while James and Ruth were playing outside,
they saw a wild pig pouting in a puddle of mud.

"Pig!" James called. "Why the long face? Why are you pouting in that
puddle of mud? You should play with us! We are running and jumping
and hiding and seeking and thanking God for the good things He made."

Pig looked up from the puddle and rolled his eyes.
"You don't *really* believe God made everything, do you?"

James and Ruth looked at each other and then looked back at Pig.
"Why wouldn't we, Pig?"

"You need a **big** imagination to believe God made everything," Pig said, as he stomped his feet in the mud. "It makes more sense to believe that everything began by accident. One day it wasn't here and then **OINK** one day it was! You see? The universe wasn't made by anyone at all."

Ruth hung her head and said, "Gee. If that's true,
I feel like pouting in a puddle of mud, too."

James nodded sadly and took Ruth's hand.
"Let's go home. I want to ask Dad about what Pig said."

That night, after they were both tucked into bed, James asked Dad about what Pig said.

"Is it silly to believe God made everything? Pig says everything
began by accident! Do you think that the universe and the sunshine
and the rain just began one day and weren't made by God at all?"

Dad listened carefully.

"Those are good questions, kiddos," Dad said, "and I'm glad you asked! It isn't silly to believe God made the universe. If your friend Pig thinks that everything began by accident and that nothing made it begin, then I'd like to know how **everything** was made by **nothing**! Can you two think of anything that has a beginning that was made from nothing, by no one, for no reason?"

James and Ruth thought about that for a long time. They couldn't think of a single thing that was made from nothing, by no one, for no reason.

"I can't think of anything like that," Ruth admitted.

"That is because everything that begins has a cause. In other words, someone or something makes it begin," Dad said. "Does your lunch make itself? Nope! Do your toys appear out of thin air?

"No way! That's just silly!" Dad exclaimed.
"Mom makes your lunch! People make toys! They
all have beginnings and they all have causes."

"So nothing in the universe is made from nothing,
by no one, for no reason?" James asked.

"That's right!" Dad said. "Everything in the universe begins because someone or something makes it begin.

"Like lunch and toys, the universe had a beginning. That means the universe had to have been caused by someone or something for some reason. The first thing the Bible tells us is that 'in the beginning God created the heavens and the earth.' So that means **God** made everything on purpose; not by accident. Isn't that amazing?

"The Bible also teaches us that God has no beginning and no end. Unlike the universe, He has always existed, and since our God has always existed, He is the only one who could have possibly made the universe begin. It sure seems like you need a big imagination to believe that God **DIDN'T** make everything!"

James fell onto his pillow. "My head is swimming, but I sure am glad God made us!"

"I don't feel like pouting in a puddle anymore!" Ruth exclaimed.

Dad laughed. "The universe and how big God
is can be hard to think about, but it is important
to know why you believe what you believe and
if what you believe is true. Goodnight, kiddos."

"Goodnight, Dad!"

That night during their prayers, James and Ruth thanked God for making everything and prayed they would remember what Dad taught them.

The next morning, James and Ruth raced back to where they'd met Pig. Pig was there, pouting in the same puddle of mud.

"Pig!" James called. "Why the long face?
Ruth and I have something to tell you."

"Everything in the universe begins because someone or something makes it begin. There is no proof that the universe itself is any different," Ruth explained. "So, since the universe had a beginning and everything that has a beginning has a cause, it isn't silly to believe that God caused the universe and everything in it to begin.

"God is the only one who could have possibly made everything in the beginning. So, now do you want to run and jump and hide and seek with us and enjoy what God made?"

James and Ruth waited excitedly for Pig to answer.
Pig looked down at the puddle, then up at them,
then down at the puddle, then up at them.

"Well, okay. Maybe just today," Pig said with a small smile.

So James and Ruth shared in all of their fun with him, and together they ran and jumped and played hide and seek and let out hollers that "God is GOOD!"

Practical Exercise

Bake some delicious chocolate chip cookies! While they are still warm, place them on a plate and sit around the plate with your family. Ask your children:

- Where do you think this cookie came from?
- Did it appear out of nowhere?
- Did someone make/create this cookie?
- How do you know this cookie was not always here?
- Is it still hot?
- Does it smell fresh?
- If it had always been here, do you think it would still be hot and still smell fresh?
- If our universe had always been here, do you think the sun would still be hot?
- Enjoy cookies and milk after you have finished discussing!

Adults,

We hear it time and time again: science has disproved the superstitious belief in God. We hear it repeated with such frequency and confidence that it begins to take root in our heart. The lie that intelligent atheism has overcome the uneducated's crutch of religious belief can begin to seem like the truth.

But what a corruption of the truth that actually is.

We Christians can have confidence that what we believe is true because there is a wealth of evidence to support our beliefs. Archaeology, history, logic, and even science, atheism's prized idol, support biblical truth in profound ways that are contrary to the taunts of the world. There is no need to make do with flimsy faith, if only we would take hold of the clues, proof, and knowledge that our Father in Heaven has given us, and that His dedicated servants have made available to us.

Our hope is that this book will help you guide your child through a simple refutation of an often repeated argument, while also equipping them to respond with courage and kindness when their beliefs are challenged. We pray that this book will inspire deep conversations between you and your child about our matchless Creator, and will encourage them to love Him in ever-deepening ways.

In Christ,
J.D. Camorlinga

THE BIG BANG IS YOUR FRIEND

The big bang theory is often regarded warily by Christians but it is actually useful evidence of creation! Study of our universe shows that it is expanding and this expansion strongly suggests that the universe had a point of origin and a cause; this fits well with the Genesis creation account. Such discoveries should not surprise us. The Bible consistently proves trustworthy under scrutiny, and science continually reveals what God's people have known for so long; His creation declares His glory! (Psalms 19:1)

THE CLASSICAL KALĀM ARGUMENT

What is the Kalām, you ask? It is an old, simple argument that logically refutes the assertion that the universe began without cause. The beauty of the Kalām is that it forces atheists to argue against the evidence given by science.

1) Everything that has a beginning of its existence has a cause of its existence;

2) The universe had a beginning of its existence;

Therefore:

3) The universe had a cause of its existence.

Stay tuned for more stories
from Picture Book Apologetics
featuring James and Ruth!

22893134R00020

Made in the USA
Charleston, SC
07 October 2013